Alexander M. Clayton

Centennial Address on the History of Marshall County

Alexander M. Clayton

Centennial Address on the History of Marshall County

ISBN/EAN: 9783337379100

Printed in Europe, USA, Canada, Australia, Japan

Cover: Foto ©ninafisch / pixelio.de

More available books at **www.hansebooks.com**

CENTENNIAL ADDRESS

ON THE

HISTORY OF MARSHALL COUNTY

DELIVERED BY

A. M. CLAYTON,

AT

HOLLY SPRINGS, MISSISSIPPI,

AUGUST 12th, 1876.

WASHINGTON, D. C.:
R. O. POLKINHORN, PRINTER.
1880.

ADDRESS.

FELLOW-CITIZENS :

I appear before you to-day, in response to your request, to deliver a lecture on the History of Marshall County. I thank you for the invitation. With me, this is a labor of love. Forty years, save two, I have lived within its borders, and borne my humble part in its struggles. After that period, full as it is of vicissitudes, wider in their range than almost any other in human experience, only a few of the early actors remain. The forms of those with whom I once associated, in the stirring scenes of busy life, and who have gone to the unknown land, flit palpably before me. We recall them for a brief moment, when we and they will alike vanish from the stage and be heard no more.

This county is just forty years old. Its name bears evidence to the deep and strong attachment of its people to the Constitution and the Union, and to the memory of the man whose genius vitalized that Constitution, and breathed into it the breath of life—John Marshall.

The territory of Mississippi was organized in 1798, and then constituted but a small part of what is now the State. Its southern boundary was the 31st parallel, its eastern the Chattahoochey river, its western the Mississippi, and a line drawn from the mouth of the Yazoo to the Chattahoochey its northern. In 1802 Georgia ceded all her lands south of the Tennessee river to the United States, and these, by an act of Congress in 1804, were attached to the Mississippi territory, which thus comprised the whole of what are now the States of Mississippi and Alabama from the 31st to the 35th parallel. The region between the 31st parallel and the Gulf was occupied by the Spaniards as our ally during the Revolutionary war, and Spain afterwards set up title to it. The Supreme Court of the United States decided this claim on the part of Spain to be invalid, and in 1811 the country below the 31st parallel, and between the Pearl and Perdido rivers, was added to the territory of Mississippi. These constituted the boundaries of the State, when it was admitted in 1817, except in the east, where the line which separates it from Alabama was established. The true location of the line of the 35th parallel, at a later day, caused some difference between this State and Tennessee, which was after the organization of this county, adjusted by a new survey. In this controversy Marshall lost a slip of valuable territory.

At the time of its admission into the Union, there were but fourteen counties, sparsely inhabited, and confined to the region bordering the old Spanish line of demarcation at 31°, and extending to the old Choctaw line. More than two-thirds of the country was in possession of the Indians, and its entire population, inclusive of the Indians, was 75,000, one-half of whom were slaves. Allured by the exuberant fertility of the soil, the people of the surrounding States flocked in and began to press upon the natives. In 1829 the legislature extended the jurisdiction of the State over all the Indian territory in its bounds, and subjected them to its laws. They became impatient of the encroachments of the whites, and of the restraints of law : and, hence, in 1830, the Choctaws, by the treaty of Dancing Rabbit Creek, and in 1832, the Chickasaws, by the treaty of Pontotoc, ceded all their remaining lands to the United States, and moved west of the Mississippi River. Almost coeval with these treaties an increased tide of population began to flow in, and a career of most unexampled prosperity was entered upon by the comers. Not only did the residents of the Southern States come to seek homes, but companies with large capital from Boston and New York made extensive investments in lands. In its native state it was a most lovely region, and no one could look on its beautiful prairies, and its forest lands covered with variegated flowers, without longing to make it his home. No wonder the Indians chanted their almost funeral dirge when they bid their last farewell to its lovely vistas.

Out of the Chickasaw Nation twelve large counties were formed by the legislature in 1836, and of these, it is but truth to say that the county of Marshall, whose history we have met to commemorate to-day, stood highest in public favor, and took the lead in numbers. In wealth, in refinement, in moral and intellectual force, whilst it challenges no preeminence over its sisters, it may at least claim equality. These newly organized counties were the most populous in the State; and her numbers gave to Marshall four members in the Lower House, and a Senator, the largest representation of any county in the State, and hence, her designation of Empire county. A distinction not always to her advantage.

The old counties of the State, seeing that power was about to pass from their hands, through their representatives in the legislature, in 1837, opposed the admission of the members from the new counties upon purely technical grounds. S. S. Prentiss, Amos R. Johnston and other distinguished men, took the lead in this opposition. It proved unavailing, and thereafter the new counties were accorded their just weight in the councils of the State. But Messrs. Prentiss, Johnston and twenty others put an earnest protest upon the journal against this action.

Marshall was never behind in her contribution of talents to the Legislature. In the earlier period of

her history, the two great political parties were so
nearly equal in strength, that the members were gen-
erally divided between them. Kyle the first Senator,
Harley, Matthews, Greer, Mason in the Senate were
always equal to the grave responsibilities which de-
volved upon them. Barton, Bradford, Hill, Josselyn,
Kemp, Holland, Autry, at one time Speaker of the
House, Thomas, Mott, Totten, Wyatt, Benton, Crump,
Withers, Malone, and a long list of other distinguished
names were honored members of the Lower House.
Mr. Totten was elected Speaker in 1844. To the
United States Senate she furnished Trotter and Chalmers, and Matthews to the office of Governor. She
sent Watson to the Confederate Senate, Clapp to the
Lower House, and Clayton to the provisional Congress. In the Supreme Court of the State, she was
represented at different times by Trotter and Clayton : in the Vice-Chancery Court by Chalmers, and
in the Circuit Court by Huling and Scruggs and Trotter.

Huling was first elected when the Judicial system
was extended to the Chickasaw counties, and was
commissioned for the "term prescribed by the constitution;" which was four years. Before the expir-
ation of that time, a general election came on, and
Howry, of LaFayette, was elected in this circuit.
Huling contested the election and refused to surrender his seat. The contest became very angry and
excited, and at the opening of Court in Holly Springs,
the first in the circuit, was very near culminating in
armed collision. The members of the bar were un-
willing to try their cases before either contestant,
they therefore made an agreed case, and referred the
decision of the controversy to the Supreme Court.
That tribunal held, that although Huling's commis-
sion called for the constitutional term of four years,
yet his time expired at the general election. The
letter of the constitution hardly warranted this de-

cision, but the spirit might, and it was made to bring about uniformity in the holding of the Judges, and to prevent a constantly recurring series of judicial elections. It met with universal acquiescence, and has furnished the unquestioned rule in subsequent cases. The ordinary routine of legislation in the State was too common-place to call forth any special notice. But in 1841 a question arose which created great agitation throughout the State, and was carried into the Legislature. That question was, as to the obligation of the State to pay the Union Bank Bonds. It was one wholly of law, and of the validity of the Bonds under the constitution. In this county, Matthews, the Senator, and Greer and Hill, two of the representatives elect, were anti-bond; Bradford and Wyatt were for their payment. The people of the State voted against their validity, and resolutions were passed by the Legislature in accordance with that vote. The members from this county voted three for—one, Bradford, against them; Wyatt absent. I do not intend to enter into the arguments on either side. I was personally in favor of their payment, and will therefore be more readily pardoned for saying, that all governments, empires, monarchies, and republics are mere corporations. The Supreme Court of the United States has time and again decided against the validity of Bonds issued by municipal corporations, cities, towns, counties, upon grounds not more strong, and objections not more forcible, than were urged against these Union Bank Bonds. The Supreme Court of our State held them to be valid and binding, but had no power to enforce its judgment. The subject has recently received a final quietus, by the enactment of a constitutional provision forbidding their payment.

The influence of the resolution of the Legislature in 1842, not to pay the Union Bank Bonds, reached far beyond what any one then dreamed of, and returned after many days to plague us, In the midst of our civil war, the Confederate Governments sent a financial agent abroad to negotiate a loan. The prospect of success in the effort was at first flattering, but the Government of the United States sent a special agent to defeat the attempt. That agent reported that President Davis was a citizen of Mississippi, and a leader in the cause of what he called repudiation, and hence asserted that any loan to the Confederate Government would be likewise repudiated. This representation, although entirely without foundation in truth, had the desired effect, the negotiation fell through, and the failure was well nigh as disastrous to the cause, as the battle of Gettysburg. Robert J. Walker, once a Senator in Congress from this State, shot this Parthian arrow.

Holly Springs, the county seat of Marshall, was incorporated in 1837. The owners of the land on which the town was located, made a donation of fifty acres to the corporation, and this sold for enough to build an excellent Court House and jail, and to lay the foundation of establishing the Holly Springs Female Institute, so long and favorably known. Its educational advantages, were from its earliest day, of a high order. This was especially true in regard to schools for girls. They extended unusual facilities for learning, under the guidance of enlightened and experienced teachers. These benefits attracted the residence of families of wealth and refinement, who came from a distance to secure the education of their children. They brought with them a high standard of religious, moral, and intellectual culture, and gave a character of unusual elevation to the place. This was so eminently the case, that in a very short time its population was over 4,000 and its real estate in demand at high prices.

The University of Holly Springs, first known as

the Holly Springs Literary Institution, was chartered in 1839, but never came up to the expectations held out by its title. With a capacity scarcely equal to that of a good grammar school, its performance fell so far short of its promise as to inflict serious injury on the place. Holly Springs would probably have been selected as the seat of the State University, if its application had not been met with the reply, you have one University, let some other place have this. Under the shadow of the State University, that at Holly Springs withered into decay, and has given place to the Chalmers Institute.

St. Thomas' Hall, a High school for boys, was established in the year 1844, by the Rev. Dr. Hawks, of the Episcopal church, founder also of an institution of the same name at Flushing on Long Island, New York. With an able and learned corps of teachers, it achieved a high reputation and attracted a large number of pupils. Whitehorn and Sears, two of its teachers, afterwards became professors in the University of this State. The former, a graduate of one of the English Universities, was the best classical scholar we have ever had amongst us. His father held a plantation in the Island of Jamaica, and was ruined by the Act of Emancipation there ; hence the son came to the South in pursuit of fortune. The latter is still Professor of Mathematics in the University of Mississippi. St. Thomas turned out many of the young men, who obtained distinction in the public service, in the last war—Walthall, Mott, Chalmers, Autry, William and Stagy Watson, Daniel Govan, Archibald McNiel, of Louisiana, Andrew and George Govan, R. S. Stith, Howard and Kinloch Falconer, Arthur Clayton, Arthur Harris, Dunlap, and three Finleys, Jos. Mayer, two Talbots, three Hollands, two Moores, Roger and Hugh Barton, Emmet and William Clayton, two Hills, Andrew Mills, and Walter Goodman. The place still maintains its high reputation for the superior excellence of its schools.

Various other places in the county have been noted for their excellent schools—Chulahoma, the Marshall Institute, Byhalia might be mentioned without intended derogation to others. Lamar should also be mentioned, founded by Spearman Holland, and deriving its name from M. B. Lamar, President of Texas.

The devotional character of its people has always been a marked feature of our Society. Churches of different denominations are scattered all over the County. They have lived on terms of entire harmony, without any of the bitter dissensions which so often agitate religious communities. No where has the great principle of religious liberty met with more unqualified recognition. In point of membership the Methodists have exceeded all others, whilst the Baptists, Presbyterians, Episcopalians, and Campbellites all have respectable followings.

Of these various denominations, men of high character and established reputation frequently had charge. Among Episcopalians at Holly Springs, the Rev. Dr. F. L. Hawks was for a time their pastor. He came here from the great city of New York, where he held distinguished position as Rector of St. Thomas' Church. He was a most polished orator, a highly cultivated scholar, and author of some literary works of acknowledged excellence. The marked feature in his character, was the graceful simplicity of his eloquence. With no high wrought periods, with no straining after effect, he could do more with a wave of his hand, or by the intonation of his voice, than other men by the most elaborate effort. He came as he said, broken with the storms of life,to seek in the comparative village of Holly Springs, the ease. and calm, and repose, which he did not findin the great Commercial Emporium. Afterwards elected Bishop of this Diocese, he was not confirmed by the House of Bishops, and his restless spirit weary of the tedium of village life, again sought companionship in wider spheres. He went to New Orleans, thence returned to New York, became pastor of Calvary church there and died in its charge. Another man of distinction who, at a later day, had charge of this church, was the Rev. Mr. Ingraham, author of the Prince of the House of David, and other works, which gave him a good deal of reputation. He was killed in the vestry room, by the accidental discharge of a pistol in his own hand, in the early period of the war.

The Presbyterian church, has likewise had men of marked piety, ability and learning, to direct its destinies. Among the first of these in every respect was the Rev. Samuel Hurd. He was a man of large acquirements, of rare excellence, and of exemplary worth, but his efficiency as pastor was greatly lessened by bad health.

The Rev. Daniel Baker, an eminent revivalist, also had charge of this church at a later day. A man of blameless life, but one who, like St. Paul says of himself, "profited above many of his equals by his exceeding zeal."

The Methodists have always been a numerous and powerful body. Many of their ministers have been men of marked ability and energy in their professions, and of earnest, high, religious and moral character. Their separation from the Northern church drove the entering wedge into the controversy which ended in civil war. This may seem strange, because their great founder, John Wesley, was one of the leading spirits of Exeter Hall, and a thorough opponent of slavery. Their struggle for religious liberty led them by an easy transition into a struggle for civil and political freedom, and shows they would not surrender their own convictions to the opinion of any leader.

The Baptists have also always maintained a high reputation for Christian virtues and unassuming piety.

The Roman Catholics, almost unknown here in the early history of the country, now have a church, with numerous members, mostly foreigners. There are but few Germans amongst them. It is a notable feature, that in the days of Luther, the Germans were in the van of the Reformation, and that they now lead the way in the march of infidelity.

The Press, next to the Pulpit, is ever the safest guardian of public morals, and best promoter and preserver of public virtue. Holly Springs has always had one or more good newspapers. The first ever published was a Democratic paper by E. Percy Howe, the name of which cannot be recalled. The editor, a sensitive, shy, retiring man was seldom seen on the streets, and known only to very few. He was a strong, original, discriminating writer, but of limited cultivation. Then there was a paper published for a short time by Patillo & Curtis, Democratic in its politics. *The Conservative*, a Whig paper, was published by Foster & Falconer, followed by the Holly Springs *Gazette* by T. A. Falconer. The first number of this paper was issued July 28th, 1841, and continued nine years. The Holly Springs *Banner*, a Whig paper, was conducted by George A. Wilson, a man of vigorous intellect and for some time District Attorney. The *Marshall Guard*, a Democratic paper, was begun first January, 1842, by Robert Josselyn—lived several years and was a highly respectable paper.

In November, 1847, the Weekly *Jacksonian* was commenced by Lloyd Selby and kept up for four years, and was succeeded by the Marshall *Jeffersonian*, with Wyatt Epps, editor, November 1851,

The first number of the Mississippi *Palladium* a Democratic States' Rights paper, was issued April 25, 1851, Henry Stith editor, Thomas A. Falconer publisher. Judge Stith was a forcible writer, with a clear conception of Constitutional law, and did good service to his party. Falconer had been an old time

Clay-whig, but when the new issues arose, he declared in favor of State Rights, and the equal right of the South in the territories. He thus became identified with the States' Rights party, and when the time came for men to show their hands, he went into the field with his two sons, and neither faltered as long as there was a flag to follow.

In 1850 the Holly Springs *Gazette* passed into new hands, with F. D. Anderson and R. S. Stith, editors and proprietors, destined to still farther changes in subsequent years.

In 1851, James W. Williams began the Marshall *Guard* which continued nearly three years.

In April, 1853, the first number of the Mississippi *Times* was issued, Samuel Benton editor and W. A. Tucker publisher; it continued to 1857. Benton was a clear, forcible writer, and intimately acquainted with the issues and questions of the day, in their minutest details. He was an old line whig, but became attached to the wing of the party known as States' Rights. He was a member of the Union convention of 1851 as well as of the Secession Convention, advocated the rights of the South in their entirety, and when the war came on, gave up his life to the cause he had so much at heart. He rose to the rank of Brigadier General before his death, and your county has testified her estimation of his worth, by giving up a large portion of her territory to a new county, bearing his name.

The distinction between the shades of southern opinion, finally became nominal rather than real; the one believing with Jefferson in the right of secession, the other with Madison in the right of Revolution, when the Constitution was persistently violated, leaving no prospect or promise of restoration. In the election for the Convention in this county, in 1860, there was only about one dozen votes of difference between the hindmost representative of the former opinion, Dr. Lea, and the foremost of the latter, Judge Watson.

In June, 1853, the Democratic *Banner* was issued by W. H. Govan, and in November 1854, the Empire *Democrat* was commenced with J. H. R. Taylor as editor. At the commencement of the war, there were three papers published here, the Southern *Herald* by Thomas A. Falconer, the *Star* by Solon L. Whittington, and the *Constitutional Union* by Upshaw & Barrett. Whittington was killed at the second battle of Fredericksburg.

Since the war there has been one or two Radical papers here, now discontinued, and the *Reporter* and the *South* still in existence, Democratic and Conservative in politics, and both maintaining a high reputation.

Another marked feature in the growth and progress of Holly Springs is the Banking system which it adopted and pursued. Two unchartered institutions, the McEwen and the McCorkle, were formed and issued a great amount of promissory notes resting for their credit upon the real estate of their members, mortgaged for their redemption, and as a consequence upon the personal liability of their Stockholders. These self-constituted Banks were formed as early as the fall of 1837 ; they applied to the Legislature for charters, failed to obtain them, and involved their members in ruinous disasters. Many of them sought refuge in Texas, to escape the results.

Strange that the history of the past, has so little influence upon the conduct of the present. The famous Mississippi scheme of John Law, which for a time held out such bright, golden visions of untold wealth, and which in its catastrophe spread unbounded ruin and dismay among its dupes, and the scarcely less famous Darien scheme of William Patterson, the founder of the Bank of England, were alike based upon the ideas of real estate security. Both were Scotchmen, and if the patronymic of our Holly Springs Bankers has not lost its significance, they too were Scotchmen by descent. This plan of Banking on a real estate capital, known in France as Credit Foncier, and that of Banking on personal estate as capital, known as credit Mobilier, have both been tried in this country unsuccessfully. But that other scheme of Scotch finance the "cash credit" system, is too refined for our practical understanding.

The Presidents of these respective institutions, McEwen and McCorkle, gave up their estates to the demands of their creditors, and preserved an unblemished reputation for integrity.

The Northern Bank of Mississippi was chartered in 1838, with its site in Holly Springs, but had too little capital to do any extensive business. Under the management of its cashier, Walter Goodman, it always maintained its credit under most trying circumstances. The present Bank maintains a high standing.

The location of the Memphis and Charleston Railroad was the cause of an angry and long continued controversy, in this and other counties. As the road of necessity must pass through a portion of this State, the county of Marshall insisted that Holly Springs should be made a fixed point in its location. The railroad company asserted that it would cause too great a deviation from a direct line, and involve an unjustifiable additional cost. For a time it seemed as if the State would refuse a charter to the company, but the county of Tishomingo consented to give a way through its borders, and the dispute was thereby settled. But it left a sting in the bosom of Holly Springs. Col. Walter, Mr. W. Goodman and others conceived the project, deemed quixotic by many, to build a railroad in the direction of New Orleans to establish communication with that city. This was the birth of the Mississippi central railroad. The enterprise was entered upon with spirit, and principally by the able speeches of Col. Walter in New Orleans, which were highly complimented at the time, and along the line of the road, the enterprise was successfully launched. A charter was obtained; by great efforts and sacrifices the stock was secured, and the plan set on foot. The Directors, most of them men of wealth, pledged their resources and their credit to the work, and through the energy and ability of their President Goodman and his co-adjutors the road was built, and is at this day operated as part of the New Orleans, St. Louis & Chicago railroad, the great route between the Lakes and Gulf.

The Mexican war forms an episode in the annals of our county and State. When it was proclaimed that our country had been invaded by a foreign foe, and American blood had been shed on American soil, the contest, under a call for volunteers, was not who should stay at home, but who should be permitted to go. On the 9th of June, 1846, the first company marched from this county, called the Marshall Guards, with A. B. Bradford as captain, J. H. R. Taylor, C. H. Mott and W. Epps, lieutenants. Robert Josselyn, Henry Trotter, son of the judge, two Yanceys, and others of our worthiest sons, were a part of its rank and file, conspicuously, Thad. L. Randolph, only 16 years of age. He was the pet of the company, and brave as a young lion, and is still living in the county of Panola. When the company reached Vicksburg it became part of the 1st Mississippi Regiment, and Captain Bradford of the Guards was elected colonel. The point was afterwards made that though he had a plurality of votes, he did not have a majority of the whole. He was legally entitled to the position, but with laudable magnanimity, he resigned and went into another election, when Jefferson Davis was elected colonel, Alex. K. McClung, lieut.-col., and Bradford, major. This company volunteered only for twelve months, but in that short period it made a record for all time. The regiment, by its brilliant achievements on every battle-field made the name of Jefferson Davis historic, and one and all have clung to his fortunes with unfaltering devotion even to this their saddest and darkest hour. It was currently said at the time that the stain of repudiation, if stain there were, had been wiped from the name of Mississippi by the heroism of her sons. Many left their bones on the plains of Mexico; some have died peacefully at home; some still live, and some, Mott notably among them, gave their lives to the Lost Cause.

The only other company from this county left in December, 1846, and constituted part of the 2d regiment, with Reuben Davis as colonel and Jos. H. Kilpatrick as lieut,-colonel. The regiment remained several weeks in New Orleans after its organization, and suffered very severely there and at other points by sickness. At Monterey both Col. Reuben Davis and Kilpatrick resigned, and Charles Clark, afterwards our Governor, and conspicuous in the civil war, was elected colonel. His battle-scarred form supported on crutches attests his bravery and suffering. The regiment remained in service only twelve months and never had the fortune to be in battle.

There were but few manufactories in the county, one of the largest and most flourishing and prosperous was the foundry of Jones, McElwain & Co.

A marble yard at which fine work is turned out, is another successful establishment. The enduring monument which the county has erected to her Confederate dead, is the work of this company, and reflects credit alike on its execution and on the generosity of those who raised it. The contribution from an exhausted and impoverished people portrays more eloquently their gratitude, than would a costlier cenotaph from a richer community. It tells of a glory, that will not grow old, and is a tribute to those who

18

fell in defense of their hearths and homes, and all
that men hold most dear.

> " They are gone to their graves grim and gory,
> The beautiful, brave and bold;
> But out of the darkness and desolation,
> Of the mourning heart of a widow'd nation,
> Their memory awaketh an exultation."

The mercantile class in the county has always been
large enough to conduct its business. The pursuit,
however, has not been conspicuously profitable. Only
the mechanic arts of the most ordinary and every
day kind have been practiced. The medical profession has been represented by skilful and efficient
practitioners : Caruthers, Gholson, Dancy, Dougherty,
Taylor, Gray, Pitman, Alexander, Mabry, Drs. G. W.
Smith, Crisp & Jamison, Sale and Webb.

Of the legal profession, it is difficult for me to
speak. An actor in many of the exciting scenes of the
forum, I saw less perhaps than a mere looker-on, and
of what I saw I may be a less impartial judge. But
the picture would be incomplete. without at least
some attempt at delineation.

At the March term, 1838, of the Circuit Court,
there were more than 1,200 cases on the docket.
The fame of this bountiful litigation drew many of
the profession here. There were over forty resident
lawyers, thrown suddenly together—there was no acknowledged leader ; and an earnest and eager com-
petition for ascendancy naturally sprang up. Some
came with established reputation ; others full of
young life and hope and ambition fighting for a career. Some succeeded. some failed ; a few brief
sketches is all that I can essay.

Parry W. Humphries, at different times a Judge
of the Circuit and Supreme Court, of Tennessee, a
member of Congress, and coming within one vote
of beating John H. Eaton for the United States Senate, was the first name in the firm of Humphreys,

Barton & Powell. He had long passed the meridian of life, and left the laborious part of the practice to the junior members of the firm.

Mr. Barton had been Prosecuting Attorney in Tennessee, was better acquainted with the criminal than with the civil law, was a strong and powerful advocate, and became the leading criminal lawyer of his day.

Alfred H. Powell was younger ; he had married the daughter of Judge Humphries, had been trained in the law school of Judge Tucker, of Virginia, had a thorough knowledge of his profession, was a pointed and effective speaker and in every respect an accomplished lawyer. He died very suddenly, leaving a high reputation for ability, and in the midst of promise of future exalted distinction.

Then there was Alex. B. Lane, profoundly versed in legal learning, a skillful advocate of singular modesty, of unblemished integrity, without guile, a sincere friend, a devout Christian ; he had an enviable standing among his peers. There were Bradford, Chalmers, Anderson, Freeman, Clapp, Craft, Lucas, Totten, Wm. Davis, the two Wilsons, McCampbell and Isaacs —killed in his office in broad daylight—all men of mark and distinction. There too was the writer of this sketch, whose place must be assigned by other hands.

Of lawyers who attended this Court from other counties, there was Wm. Y. Gholson, of Pontotoc, the equal of any ; he afterwards went to Ohio and became one of the Supreme Judges of that state ; Jacob Thompson, Secretary of the Interior under Buchanan, and T. Jeff. Word, the colleague of S. S. Prentiss in Congress, and in his famous contest with Claiborne and Sam Gholson for a seat in the House. At a later day there was Larmar, the present distinguished member of Congress.

I have reserved for the last, the name of William

F. Stearns, my friend, pupil in law, my partner, my successor to my practice. A clear, acute, incisive intellect, rather than brilliant or showy. Patient, industrious, methodical, he could dispatch a vast amount of business without display of labor. He became Professor of Law, at the State University, performed its duties with universal acceptance, and was beloved and respected beyond measure.

In the discussion which preceded the civil war, his pen was active in advocacy of the principles for which the South contended. He wrote especially one article to prove that the Federal government had no constitutional right or power to coerce a State by force. That article was placed in the hands of Mr. Buchanan, the then President, by a member of his cabinet, after his last message had been written. It changed his views, he adopted its reasoning, and in his latest authoritative utterance propounded the State Rights' doctrine, *that Congress could not coerce a State.* A politician, high in the ranks of the radical party, for that message said. "that Jefferson Davis was an angel of light compared to James Buchanan." Would to God that other intellects could have been opened to conviction, ere the flood-gates of blood and of carnage were let loose on the land. Alas, that such a mind as that of Stearns, should have been clouded by despair and despondency, and that weary of life, he should have cast it away by his own hand. If you mourn that mental powers of the highest order—that purity of heart, and kindness of feeling could not save him from great and grievous error;

> "Be every harsher thought supprest,
> And sacred be his last, long rest."

Of the present members of the profession, this is not the time to speak in detail, though some of them run back into "auld lang syne." Some of them, Watson, now Judge, Walter, Featherston, Harris,

Stith, Strickland, may claim to have gained "that clear conception of the law, the attainment of which, Mr. Buckle thinks, is the highest point the human intellect can reach."

We come now to speak briefly of the advance of the county in population and wealth.

In 1840, its population, according to the United States census, was 17,526; in 1850; 29,689; in 1860, 28,823; in 1870, 29,416; its proportion of slaves in each instance, except the first and last, being a little more than half. It has always been principally an agricultural, not a manufacturing or commercial community. Cotton has been its chief product. The number of bales grown in 1840 I do not find reliably reported; in 1850 it was 32,775. and in 1860, 49,348, enough to have insured prosperity and abundant comfort to every inhabitant, and the largest number of bales raised by any county in the United States.

And here I wish the curtain could fall upon a peaceful, prosperous and happy people ; but the truth of history will not permit this.

"From soul to soul hath war been waged,
From star to star, from sun to sun;
Nor e'er shall be the strife assuaged,
That's hourly lost and hourly won."

Our beloved country forms no exception to this stern lesson of the past.

It was the fond dream of the framers of the Federal Constitution that they formed a government for all time to come, sufficient in itself for its own protection and perpetuity, and the preservation of all rights which fell within it. Slavery was known to exist, as an element of discord, but it was believed not to be of a character which would make permanent harmony impracticable. It had been introduced by the English government into the colonies. against their remonstrance—established by law—recognized in the constitution as existing and established—provision made therein for its protection—the African slave trade permitted to be continued for a time for the benefit of the shipping and commercial interests, and its existence regarded as a source of wealth. The feeling against it increased in intensity. In 1820 it excited an alarm, as Mr. Jefferson said, like a fire-bell at night. It was then quieted by the Missouri compromise, to be renewed at intervals with ever-growing bitterness. It pervaded the pulpits dedicated to God; it moved the ministers of religion, as if their mission was not to bring peace into the world, but a sword —it entered the Legislative halls it stirred up the people at the polls, and finally invaded the Courts of the country. It was still hoped that the Constitution was equal to the strain. It had formed a system of co-ordinate government, combining two different sources of power, Federal and State, each supreme in its sphere, and each virtually forbidden to intrude on the sphere of the other. "The one supreme for National purposes, and the State governments in many respects independent, for other purposes." It had instituted a supreme court, aptly described as a more than Amphyctionic council, to decide between the conflicts of varying legislation and whose decisions on matters within its jurisdiction, were to be final and conclusive on all. By the decisions of this tribunal, a perfect theory of the working of the government was evolved. This Court could decide both Acts of Congress and State laws to be unconstitutional. The States could not invade the domain of the Federal government, and by reciprocal rule that government could not trench upon the powers of the States, and thus all the functions of government, foreign and domestic, National and State were to be carried on in harmony and without jar. It constituted a frame of government, *totus teres et rotundus*, entire, complete and rounded off in symmetry, with a capacity to last forever if its established harmonies were preserved.

23

Such were the teachings of Marshall, the almost inspired oracle of the constitution—such were the decisions of the Court during his time, and the influence of his name gave them unquestioned authority during his life. After his death the judgements of the Court were less regarded, and especially was this the case in the matter of slavery. "The higher law" was invoked, and more than one name was made famous by denunciation of all the compromises of the constitution on this subject. Its admitted and undeniable provision, the enactments of State statutes, the decisions of the Supreme Court were alike disregarded, and the personal liberty laws of the anti-slave States were permitted to over-ride every other consideration. The fugitive slave laws of Congress, notwithstanding the Supreme Court had decided them to be constitutional, were evaded or openly set aside, and slavery was excluded from the territories, although the Supreme Court decided "that Congress had no power to make any difference between slave and other property, and by the constitution was bound to protect slavery." This was the state of things, property to the value of four thousand millions of dollars was involved, and to discover some remedy against its total loss, was the problem forced on the consideration of the South.

Ellsworth, a member of the convention which framed the constitution of the United States, and a member of the convention of Connecticut which ratified it, said, in the last named convention, "this Constitution does not attempt to coerce sovereign bodies—States in their political capacities—it only acts upon delinquent individuals." He was afterwards Chief Justice of the United States, and left no utterance which contradicts this expression. The constitution was a contract which derived its binding force from the accession of nine States: Virginia made the ninth accession and thus gave life to the instrument.

The exposition of this instrument made by the tribunal which was its authorized interpreter had been habitually violated by the non-slave holding States. A contract broken by one side was not binding on the other. After the union between England and Scotland, when in the opinion of the latter, the "fundamental conditions" on which the Union was formed had been broken, some of her statesmen took the ground that Scotland being an independent nation when the treaty was formed, "could henceforth resume her ancient rights." The writers on the law of Nations are uniform in declaring the same principle ; American jurists of the highest character have asserted it. And to show that the military understanding of the principle accords with the views of civilians, Gen. Sherman, the commander-in-chief of the armies of the United States, under the President, in a letter to the Secretary of War in September, 1868, in regard to the Indians says : "The treaty having been clearly violated by the Indians themselves, this hunting right is entirely lost to them, if we so declare it."

The same principle runs thro' all private transactions. If a State grants a charter to a corporation, upon a breach of the charter in a material point, the State at its pleasure may resume the grant. If individuals make a contract, upon a violation by one, the other may at his option refuse to be longer bound by it. With this concurrence of opinion in regard to National and Municipal law, if the States had formed the government by accession, the question was presented, whether they might not withdraw by secession. Most momentous results were bound up in the issue, and the best intellects of the land were enlisted in its discussion and decision.

In October, 1849, Mississippi made her first movement in the matter. A large meeting of influential citizens, mostly from the central and southern portions of the State, was held in Jackson. In this meeting your county had no part. It recommended a convention of the Southern States, to be called to consider of the situation. The Legislature of the State which assembled soon afterwards approved the plan and elected delegates to the convention, which was to meet at Nashville. Two citizens of Marshall were elected as delegates, Gov. Matthews and Judge Clayton. Mr. Word was also a member of the convention, but whether from this county I do not now remember. The convention met at Nashville in June, 1850, and was organized by the election of Judge Sharkey as President. It was attended by members from almost every Southern State. The address with the resolutions, which were finally passed, was drawn up by Judge Cheves, of South Carolina, and was directed only to the Southern States. This was not satisfactory to the delegation from Mississippi, and Judge Clayton from this county was selected to prepare an address to all the States. It was prepared and submitted to the convention, and was earnestly supported by Gov. Matthews and others, It proposed, first a convention of the Southern States, to determine what would be satisfactory to the South, and then a joint convention of all the States of the Union to consider what might be submitted by the South, and to make terms of adjustment. This address was rejected in convention, but directed to be published among its proceedings. The measure adopted by the Nashville convention, as the basis of settlement, was the extension of the Missouri compromise line to the Pacific ocean. This, however, was not accepted by Congress, and the passage of the compromise laws soon afterwards by that body was all that it did.

These compromise measures became the subject of heated and animated controversy throughout the South, and in this State, the contest assumed such large proportions, that a convention was called, and an election for members held in September, 1851.

The practical question at issue was acquiescence, or non-acquiescence in those measures. The majority in the State in favor of accepting them as a final settlement was about seven thousand. In this county Watson, Scruggs, Phillips and Benton, in favor of acquiescence, were elected over Barton, Clapp, Matthews and Crump by an average majority of 200.

In consequence of this result Gov. Quitman, who was a candidate for re-election, against General Foote who was the candidate on the side of acquiescence, withdrew from the canvass, and notwithstanding the result in the election for the convention, Jefferson Davis was placed upon the ticket in his stead. This election came off in November, 1851, and Davis was defeated by a majority of less than one thousand in the State, and carried this county by a majority of thirty votes.

The Convention met in November, 1851, and amongst other things resolved, "that the asserted right of secession was utterly unsanctioned by the Federal Constitution," but "in case of intolerable oppression, the State might resort to measures of resistance" and then follows a list of the violations which would justify resistance.

Before the election between Foote and Davis came off, the election in Georgia, in which the same matter was in issue, took place, and resulted in favor of Howell Cobb, the Union candidate. That gave the key to the election in all the Southern States, and the compromise measures were thus accepted as the final adjustment of the troubles.

Then came a lull in the tempest for a short time, though accompanied by almost continued agitation in Congress. The Missouri compromise law was repealed, a determined disposition was manifested to confine slavery to existing limits, and thus to put it in "the gradual process of extinction."

The election of Mr. Lincoln, by which the two

most powerful departments of the government, were
secured to the anti-slavery party, and the utter dis-
regard of the decision of the Supreme court as to the
duty of Congress to protect slavery, determined the
South again to come together for consultation. It
was admitted that no league or confederation could
be formed by any part of the States, while they remained in the Union, without a violation of the Federal
constitution. Hence it was determined first to hold
State conventions, to secede if deemed best, and then
to hold a general convention of the Southern States.
The legislature of this State, at its special ses-
sion in November, 1860, passed an act calling a convention, and providing for the payment of its ex-
penses. An election was held under this law, and
Marshall county chose as her delegates Samuel Benton, J. W. Clapp, A. M. Clayton, W. M. Lea, and H.
W. Walter. This convention met at Jackson in January, 1861, and on the 9th day of the month passed
an ordinance of secession. All the members from
this county voted for it, with a deep conviction of
the vast responsibility it involved, but a still deeper
conviction of its necessity, if the doctrine of State
Rights, was not to be abandoned, and the immense
value of slave property was not to be given up. The
convention also decided to send delegates to the general convention of the Southern States, to be held at
Montgomery, Alabama, and elected Judge Clayton
of your county, as one of its members. The convention met in Montgomery, Alabama, on the 4th of Feb-
ruary, 1861, and by the 8th had prepared a Provisional Constitution for the government of the
Confederate States. It organized a regular government, and proceeded to enact laws suited to the press-
ing emergencies of the occasion. It was shortly after declared that by acts of the government of the
United States, war existed between that government
and the Confederate States, and every available prep-

aration made for its conduct. And in the language of the Supreme Court of the United States, "this greatest of civil wars sprung forth at one bound in the full panoply of war." After the adjournment of the convention and of Congress, your member returned, and submitted his action to the State convention which had again met at Jackson, and that action was approved by it. He also submitted it to his more immediate constituents of this county, who likewise put their seal of approbation upon it.

This record is made here in your behalf, that the reasons which guided our conduct may be known to an impartial future, and that any who desire to investigate our course may here find the means of investigation and judgment. It is made with no wish to kindle anew the fires of discord, or to re-open the wounds of past dissension:

It is far from my purpose to attempt even the faintest sketch of the battles of the war. As your county had always been prompt in the assertion of her rights, she was equally prompt and persistent in their maintenance. Scarce a prominent battle-field that is not blood-stained by the track of your sons. In four months from the opening of the war you had sent seven companies to the front : the Home Guards, Capt. Thos. W. Harris ; the Jeff. Davis Rifles, Capt. Sam. Benton ; the Quitman Guards, Cap. Robt. McGowan ; all leaving March 28, 1861, for Pensacola. Then the Confederate Guards, Capt. W. S. Featherston, the Mississippi Rangers, a company of beardless boys, Capt. John McGuirk ; Marshall Rifles, Capt. T. J. Hardin ; and the Sam. Benton Rifles, Capt. W. T. Ivy. Then followed the Mott Rifles, Capt. Gaston Martin ; the Rough and Ready, Capt. Henry E. Williamson ; the Goodman Guards, T. A. Falconer and Bernard Brown's company, Captain Webbers' Cavalry Company, with others constantly going out during the war.

Where there are so many entitled to distinction, it is not an easy or a pleasant task to discriminate, and whilst I can name but a comparative few, I wish some one else would make a complete list of those who rose to high rank.

W. S. Featherston, A. J. Vaughan, H. W. Walter, Clifton Dancy, Geo. Myers, T. A. Falconer and his two sons Howard and Kinloch Falconer, A. T. Mason, Thos. W. Harris still survive ; Benton, Mott, Autry, C. G. Nelms, Andrew Govan, Hardin, Barksdale, Braden, Webber, Bernard Brown and H. J. Bowen fell on the battle field. Of those less in rank, but not less in devotion to their country, there were Roger Barton, five Crumps, four Leas, two Watsons, ten Claytons. seven Fants. five Morgans, three Hollands, ten Rogers, five Myers, four Dancys, four Treadwells, three Walthalls, two Marshes, two Glenns, two Chalmers, two McWilliams, four Browns, six Jones, three Powells, Sims, Baum, McKie, Cyrus Johnson, Andrew Jackson, R. S. Stith, Withers, four Govans and four Andersons. Of these Roger Barton, two Leas, sons of Dr. Willis M. Lea, two Watsons, sons of Judge Watson, two Fants, sons of Col. J. W. Fant, two Andersons and Cyrus Johnson were killed in battle, and with a long list of others, form a holocaust of victims never to be forgotten by you, whilst a soul survives of the days of 1861. The flowers that are yearly strewn upon their graves, show that their memories are still fresh and green as those flowers, in the hearts of the survivors.

In the iron storm of battle, in the gloom of the midnight march, amid the ice and snows of winter, under the burning rays of a vertical sun, over rivers and over mountains, in hunger and in want, they exhibited a heroism and patience under suffering, and a perseverance under misfortune, that could not be surpassed.

Not the heroes of the Revolution. the followers and

the soldiers of Washington endured or did more than your sons and brothers under the lead of Lee. The one is immortal in the burning light of victory, the other no less immortal, in the gloom and shadow of defeat.

" 'Tis a cause, not the *fate* of a cause, that is glorious."

At the close of the war the South was utterly exhausted. Its supplies of men, of money, of clothing and provisions were gone. In destitution, in poverty, in suffering, and in sorrow, there was nothing left but to bow to fate, and to lay the foundations of a new fortune. As some illustration of the situation let us contrast two States, at the beginning and after the close of the war : Massachusetts and Mississippi. The census returns for 1860 gave Massachusetts a sum total of wealth of $777,157,816, and in 1870. of $1,361,166,403 ; gain in 10 years, including war, $584,011,587. The same document gives Mississippi for 1860 a total wealth of $509,448,912 ; in 1870, of 154,535,557 ; loss in same ten years, $353,937,355.

Surely this great loss on the part of a once noble State, ought to be sufficient to satisfy the most insatiate appetite for punishment, and to induce the feeling that henceforth the effort should be to help her to rise.

That the effects of emancipation were not unlookeed for, it may be permitted to advert to the fact that in an address to the people of this State in 1850, from the same hand that pens this sketch, it was told "that the abstraction of so much capital from the commerce of the world would derange every branch of business —agricultural, commercial and manufacturing— throughout Christendom." Is not this anticipation amply fulfilled at this time in the prostrate condition of every branch of industry throughout the world.

Macauly says that after the last civil war in England. English dukes were seen in the streets of cities on the Continent, barefooted and bareheaded, begging alms. The great disposer of events saved us from this deep humiliation. Our people sought redemption in their own unconquered energy. Work was one of the inspirations of the hour; there was another not less potent: *Woman.* Woman, on whom the result bore more heavily than on the men, wasted no thoughts on fortunes changed, and uttered no vain regrets or useless repinings; but set to work to revive the drooping spirits of fathers, husbands, brothers, sons, and did all in their power to aid, comfort and sustain them. Who could falter or despond with such examples of courage and fortitude before them.

> "All honor to women, to them it is given,
> To garland the earth with the roses of heaven."

We have bowed in silent submission and acquiescence to the arbitrament of war:—we have neither the wish nor the power to disturb it. Our desire is to be allowed to go forward and aid in the full development of the riches and the resources of this great nation, praying that it may be one in harmony of all its interests, and one in the grand endeavor to elevate the cause of humanity in all its domains.

In the language of one of the most gifted writers of New England: "We look not mournfully into the past, it comes not back again. We strive to improve the present, it is ours. We go forth to meet the future, without fear, and with a manly heart."

My task is done. Spirit of Marshall! you, whose name we bear, the foremost name in the annals of American jurisprudence if not of the world, you who saw through the constitution, with a mental vision so clear, that it swept away all obscurities, we appeal to you, if we did not follow your judgments as the authorized and conclusive exposition of the constitution, until the sword was thrown into the scale, and the dogmas of force substituted for the conclusions of reason, and whether if others who were bound by the same ties, had yielded the same obedience to the Supreme laws as inculcated in your decisions the country would not have been saved from the deluge of civil war, and the unnumbered woes which have followed in its train.

www.ingramcontent.com/pod-product-compliance
Lightning Source LLC
Chambersburg PA
CBHW021457090426
42739CB00009B/1763

* 9 7 8 3 3 3 7 3 7 9 1 0 0 *